First Facts®

The Solar System

Asteroids, Comets, and Meteorites

by Steve Kortenkamp

Consultant:
James Gerard
Aerospace Education Specialist, NASA
Kennedy Space Center, Florida

Capstone
press®

Mankato, Minnesota

First Facts is published by Capstone Press,
151 Good Counsel Drive, P.O. Box 669, Mankato, Minnesota 56002.
www.capstonepress.com

Library of Congress Cataloging-in-Publication Data
Kortenkamp, Steve.
 Asteroids, comets, and meteorites / by Steve Kortenkamp.
 p. cm.—(First facts. The solar system)
 Summary: "Describes the small solar system bodies asteroids, comets, and
meteorites"—Provided by publisher.
 Includes bibliographical references and index.
 ISBN-13: 978-1-4296-0059-0 (hardcover)
 ISBN-10: 1-4296-0059-4 (hardcover)
 1. Asteroids. 2. Comets. 3. Meteorites. I. Title. II. Series.
QB651.K665 2008
523.2—dc22   2006100041

Editorial Credits
Jennifer Besel, editor; Juliette Peters, set designer; Patrick D. Dentinger, book designer; Jo Miller,
  photo researcher

Photo Credits
Digital Vision, 10
iStockphoto/Michael Puerzer, 1
NASA Johnson Space Center, 16; JPL, cover (asteroid), 8, 9, 19; JPL/Cornell, cover (meteorite)
Photodisc, cover (comet), 21
Photo Researchers, Inc/David Hardy, 13; Detlev van Ravenswaay, 6; Frank Zullo, 5; John R.
  Foster, 14–15
University of Alabama Museums, Alabama Museum of Natural History, Tuscaloosa, Alabama, 20
Visuals Unlimited/Paul Bierman, 17

1 2 3 4 5 6 12 11 10 09 08 07

Table of Contents

Studying the Solar System

We have lots of questions about our solar system. How did the planets form? Is there life in outer space? Astronomers study the solar system to find answers to our questions. But planets aren't the only things they study. Asteroids, comets, and meteorites also contain information about our big, mysterious solar system.

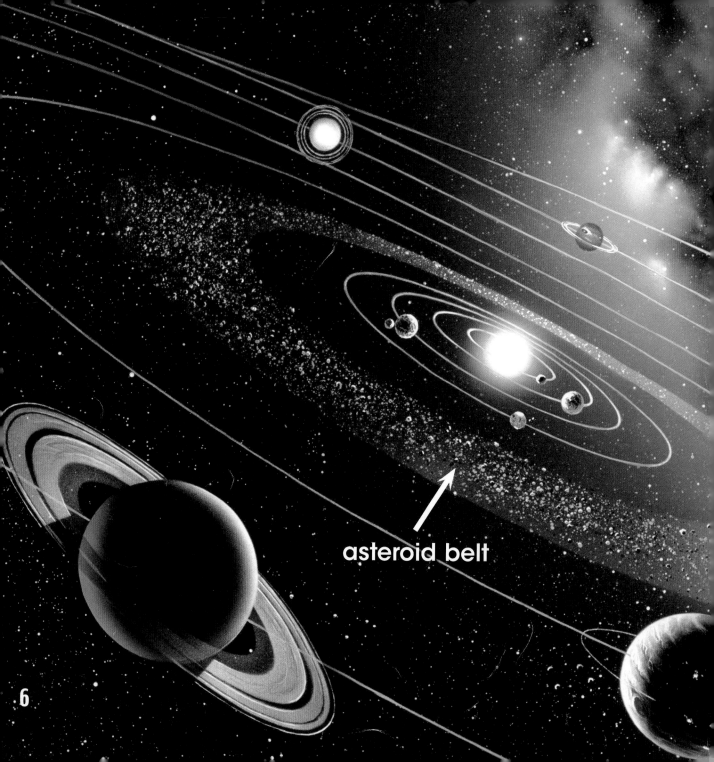

asteroid belt

Asteroids

Millions of rocky objects **orbit** the Sun. Scientists call these objects asteroids. Asteroids are really leftover material from when the planets formed billions of years ago.

The area between Mars and Jupiter is home to most asteroids. This space is called the **asteroid belt**.

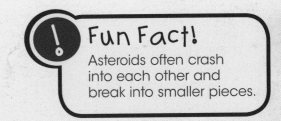

Fun Fact!
Asteroids often crash into each other and break into smaller pieces.

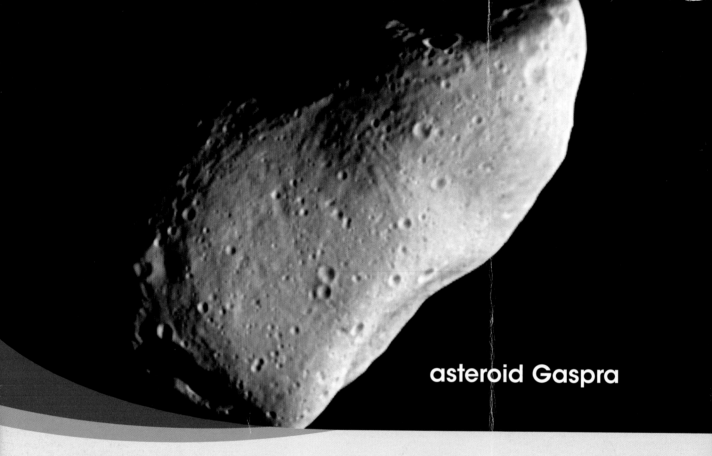

asteroid Gaspra

What Asteroids Look Like

No two asteroids are the same. Some are no bigger than a house. Others are so big they look like planets. The biggest asteroid is almost the size of Texas.

In 1993, a **spacecraft** took pictures of an asteroid named Ida. Astronomers saw that Ida is covered in holes. Like Ida, most asteroids have many **craters**.

asteroid Ida

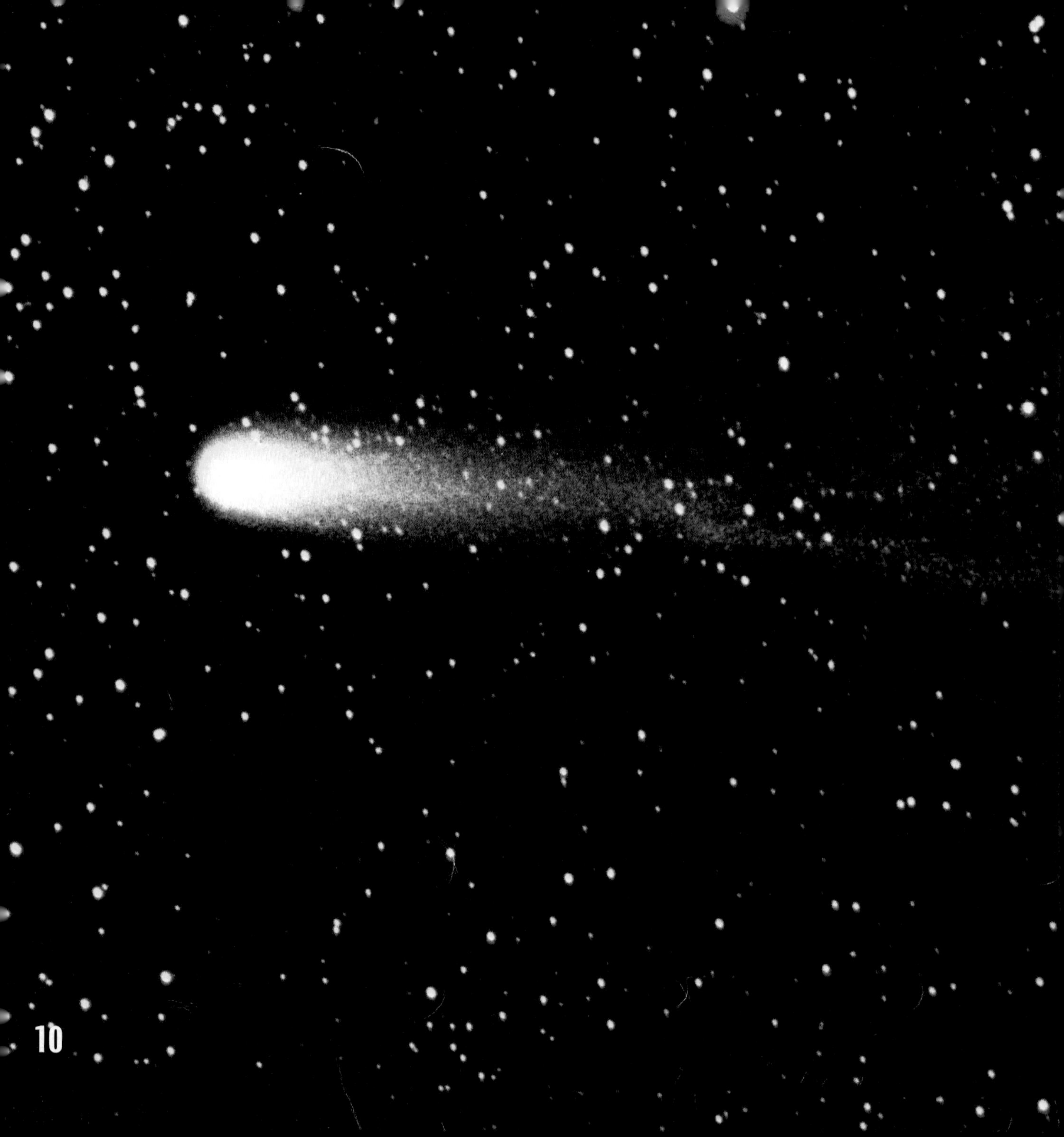

Comets

Past Neptune there are many icy rocks. Once in a while, one of these rocks gets too close to the planet. Neptune's **gravity** swings the rock into orbit around the Sun. As it nears the Sun, sunlight pushes gas and dust off the rock. A long tail forms. The rock is now a comet.

Fun Fact!
Comet tails can stretch across space for millions of miles.

How Comets Move

Comets move around the Sun in stretched-out paths. Some take a few years to go around, while others take thousands of years. Comets grow new tails each time they get near the Sun.

One of the most famous comets is Halley's comet. It gets near the sun every 76 years. Maybe you'll see it when it returns in 2062.

Fun Fact!
Gravity from the Sun makes comets move very fast when they are close to it, but very slow when they are far away.

one comet's orbit

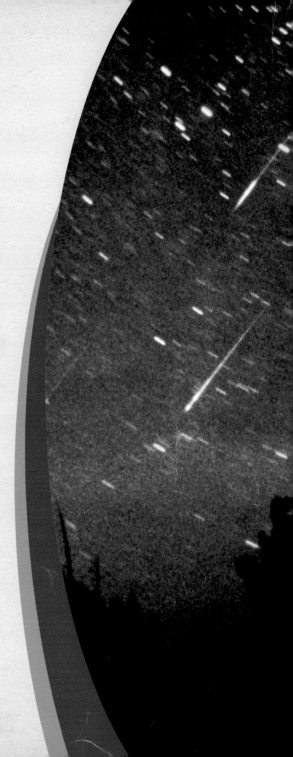

Meteors

On most nights, you'll see a few flashes of light in the sky. These flashes are meteors. Meteors happen when pieces from asteroids and comets burn up in Earth's **atmosphere**.

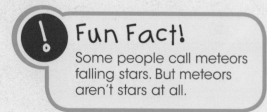

! Fun Fact!
Some people call meteors falling stars. But meteors aren't stars at all.

Meteorites

Some rocks from space are too big to totally burn up in Earth's atmosphere. These rocks hit the ground and are called meteorites.

Meteorites come in all sorts of
shapes and sizes. The smallest ones are
as small as grains of sand. The largest
meteorite ever found is as big as a car.

the Hoba meteorite in Namibia, Africa

17

Searching for Clues

Astronomers study space objects to learn how the solar system formed. In 2003, a spacecraft collected dust from a comet. Astronomers found that the dust had been hot before it was frozen inside the comet. They aren't sure how this happened. But they hope information like that will one day help them solve the mysteries of the solar system.

Amazing but True!

Meteorites fall from space every day. Every once in a while, a meteorite falls in an area where people live. One meteorite came through the roof of a house in Alabama and landed on a woman's leg. Another landed right at the feet of two boys playing in their yard in Indiana. Others have hit cars, houses, and even a horse.

Think Big!

The dinosaurs went extinct 65 million years ago. Some scientists think this happened because a big asteroid hit our planet. We don't want the same thing to happen again. So astronomers are searching for asteroids that might hit Earth in the future. If they find one coming, can you think of a good way to stop it?

Glossary

asteroid belt (AS-tuh-roid BELT)—the area in space between Mars and Jupiter where the most asteroids are found

atmosphere (AT-muhss-feehr)—the mixture of gases that surrounds some planets and moons

crater (KRAY-tur)—a hole made when large pieces of rock crash into the surface of a planet, moon, or asteroid

gravity (GRAV-uh-tee)—a force that pulls objects together

orbit (OR-bit)—to circle another object in space

spacecraft (SPAYSS-kraft)—a vehicle that travels in space

Read More

Bell, Trudy E. *Comets, Meteors, Asteroids, and the Outer Reaches*. The New Solar System. Mankato, Minn.: Smart Apple Media, 2003.

Mist, Rosalind. *Could an Asteroid Hit the Earth? Asteroids, Comets, Meteors, and More*. Stargazers Guides. Chicago: Heinemann, 2006.

Rau, Dana Meachen. *Space Leftovers: A Book about Comets, Asteroids, and Meteoroids*. Amazing Science. Minneapolis: Picture Window Books, 2006.

Internet Sites

FactHound offers a safe, fun way to find Internet sites related to this book. All of the sites on FactHound have been researched by our staff.

Here's how:
1. Visit *www.facthound.com*
2. Choose your grade level.
3. Type in this book ID **1429600594** for age-appropriate sites. You may also browse subjects by clicking on letters, or by clicking on pictures and words.
4. Click on the **Fetch It** button.

Facthound will fetch the best sites for you!

Index